OCEANS ALIVE!

The Deep, Deep Ocean

BROWN
BEAR
BOOKS

Published by Brown Bear Books Limited

An imprint of
The Brown Reference Group Ltd
68 Topstone Road
Redding
Connecticut
06896
USA
www.brownreference.com

© 2009 The Brown Reference Group Ltd

Library of Congress Cataloging-in-Publication
Data available on request.

ISBN-13: 978-1-933834-63-4

Printed in the United States of America

For The Brown Reference Group Ltd
Project Editor: Tom Jackson
Designer: Lynne Lennon
Picture Researcher: Sean Hannaway
Indexer: Tom Jackson
Design Manager: David Poole
Managing Editor: Tim Harris
Production Director: Alastair Gourlay
Children's Publisher: Anne O'Daly
Editorial Director: Lindsey Lowe

Picture Credits
Front Cover: Photoshot: Oceans Image/Norbert
Wu c; Shutterstock: Chad McDermott t,
Irabel8 b.

Corbis: Julie Houck 9t, Jeffrey Rotman 6-7, Ralph
White 8, 22-23, 24-25; FLPA: Chris Newbert 14-
15, Norbert Wu 4b, 16, 17t, 19; Getty Images:
Bill Curtsinger 11, Popperfoto 23; iStockphoto:
Phill Danze 24, Klaas Lingbeek van Kranen 7, Lee
Pettet 9b, Pomortzeff 12, Snaprender 13b;
Jupiter Images: 13t; NASA: JPL 10; Natural
Visions: Heather Angel 27, Peter David 17b, 18,
21b, 29; Nature PL: Doug Perrine 20; NOAA: 28;
PA Photos: AP/Tsunemi Kubodera/National
Science Museum of Japan 21t; Science Photo
Library: USGS 26; Shutterstock: Irabel8 1b, 3b,
Chad McDermott 1t, 3t, Armin Rose 14,
WebStudio24h 4t, Vling 5.

Artworks: The Brown Reference Group Ltd.

Contents

Introduction

Less than a thousand feet below the surface, the ocean becomes a dark and cold place, almost cut off from the surface.

Down below

At the surface, the ocean often looks different. Some areas are clear and calm, while others are tossed by tall waves. But these differences disappear deep beneath the surface. The water there is always calm. Surface winds that whip up waves have no effect below 330 feet (100 meters). It is also cold. Even the hottest sunshine warms only the top 800 feet (240 meters).

Into the dark

Deep water also loses its color. Below 600 feet (180 meters), the only light is a faint blue glow, like you get at **twilight**. The glow soon fades and even in clear water it is totally dark below 3,300 feet (1,000 meters)—even at midday. This is the start of the **midnight zone,** and it stays dark all the way to the bottom.

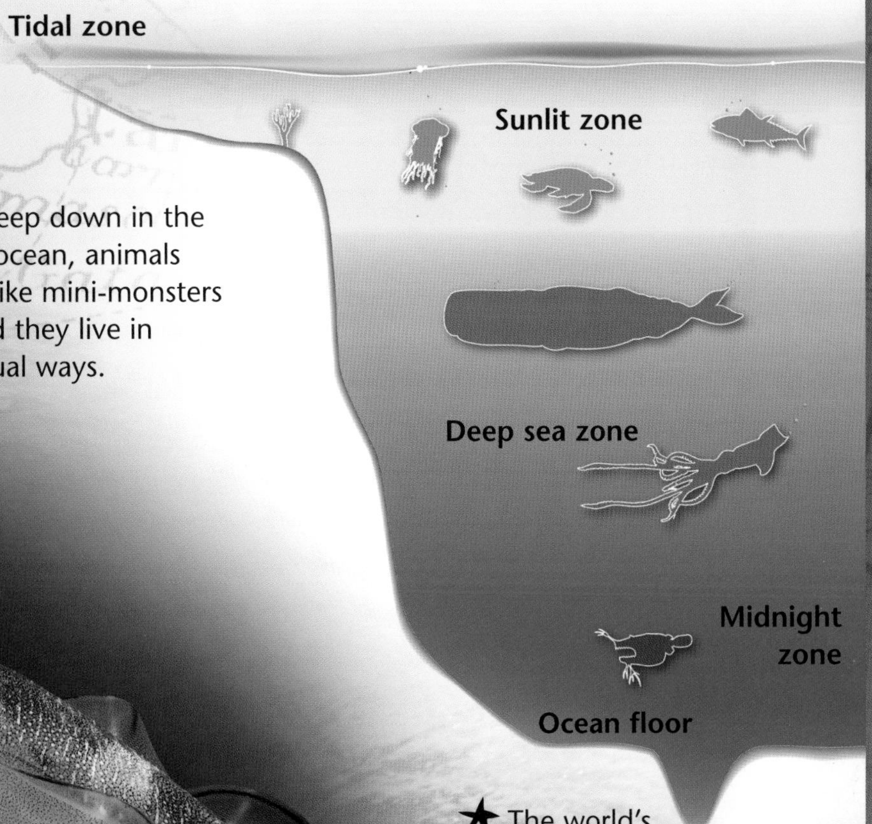

Tidal zone

Sunlit zone

★ Deep down in the dark ocean, animals look like mini-monsters —and they live in unusual ways.

Deep sea zone

Midnight zone

Ocean floor

★ The world's oceans can be divided into zones. Each one has a certain set of conditions.

★ MUCH TO LEARN

The dark depths make up about three-quarters of the world's ocean water. They account for more than half of the total living space on Earth! Yet we know very little about them. For every animal that we know about down there, there are probably 100 that we do not know.

Your Mission

To find out what is hiding in the deep oceans, you will have to make the dangerous journey into the dark waters. Good luck!

★ A submersible is the only way to visit the deep ocean. It is too far to swim!

Into the unknown

A person cannot visit the deep ocean without a special submarine, known as a **submersible**. A submersible is like an underwater spacecraft, and your mission will be like a flight into space. Scientists actually know more about the surface of the Moon or Mars than they do about what is in the deep ocean here on Earth!

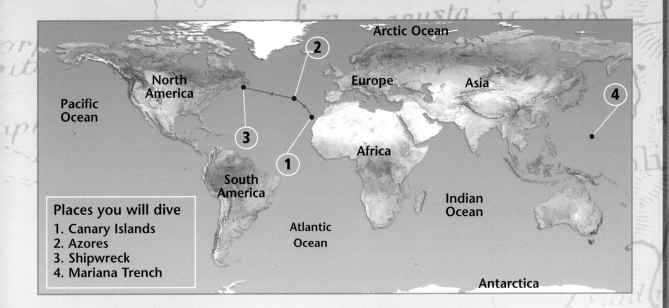

Arctic Ocean

North America

Europe

Asia

Pacific Ocean

4

3

1

Africa

South America

Indian Ocean

Atlantic Ocean

Antarctica

Places you will dive
1. Canary Islands
2. Azores
3. Shipwreck
4. Mariana Trench

Straight down

Your mission into the deep starts in the Atlantic Ocean. You will start by investigating the weird animals that survive in darkness. You will also look at a shipwreck lying in deep water to see what happens to human-made objects down there. Finally, you will go to the Pacific and take a dive into the deepest ocean of all.

★ People are not the only air-breathing animals that visit the midnight zone. Sperm whales dive down there looking for food.

Aboard the Sub

A submersible is a tough machine. It must be strong enough to survive the huge crushing forces in the deep ocean. And it must also be highly mobile so it can move in all directions in the empty water.

Safe sphere

The crew sit inside a **pressure**-proof chamber. The strongest shape for this is a thick ball, or sphere. Any doors are made so that the **water pressure** squeezes them shut—so the deeper you go, the harder they are to open. The windows are made of thick plastic.

★ Mechanical arms on the front of the sub collect samples and put them in a sample basket.

★ The sub's plastic windows are thicker than the walls of your house.

Self-contained

The crew spend the voyage inside an air-filled cabin. The air supply is stored in smaller tanks next to the main cabin. Small electric motors called thrusters are hung on the outside. Some point forward and back, but others point sideways, or up and down. Between them, they can push the sub in any direction.

★ EMERGENCY! 🐟

If the sub's engine or the steering controls fail, the submersible will begin to sink—and then crash or be crushed! However, the submersible has an escape system. The main sphere breaks away from the rest of the craft and floats back to the surface with the crew inside.

Crush-proof

During the dive, the cabin is kept dark to save power. When the sub reaches its destination bright lights are switched on outside to show what is there. The lights have to be especially strong. Normal light bulbs would shatter even in shallow water. The sub's cameras are also encased inside thick metal and plastic to keep the cold and water pressure from damaging the electronics.

Visitor in the Dark

Your first dive will be near the coast of Tenerife, the largest of the Canary Islands. You set off from the port at dusk, and you soon see that you are not the only ship on the move.

On the move

Tenerife fishing boats follow your research vessel as you head to deep water. The fishers are heading out now because they catch more fish at night. Deep-water fish come closer to the surface when it is dark up top.

Dark waters

While the fishers lower their nets, your submersible is hoisted over the side. Soon you are traveling into the darkness. It is night at the surface, and the pilot turns the sub's lights on straight away. You see some strange fish. Many of them glow with their own faint light. Next you see a large fish being attacked by a small shark. The attacker is a cookie-cutter shark. Its belly glows with a faint green light.

★ Tenerife is the tip of an **extinct** volcano that rises more than 23,000 feet (7,000 meters) from the seabed.

Edge of the deep

You follow the shark down to 3,300 feet (1,000 meters). That is the top of the midnight zone—and deep enough for now. But the shark keeps on going and soon disappears in the dark water. What else is down there?

★ Cookie-cutter sharks are named for the way that they bite circular, cookie-shaped chunks out of larger fish.

The Big Squeeze

Now you are down in the deep ocean, you use your submersible's sensors to measure the conditions. You are amazed anything can live down there!

Pushing down

Water is heavy. Just try lifting a bucket of water. The ocean is incredibly heavy and all that weight presses down on the ocean floor. A sensor on your sub has measured the pressure as you dived. At 3,300 feet (1,000 meters), the pressure is more than 100 times greater than at the surface.

★ A jellyfish is 90 percent water. Why is its body not crushed in deep water?

Liquid protection

Pressure like that is enough to squash you into mush. How do deep-sea animals survive? Their bodies are full of water. Water is a liquid and does not shrink when it is squeezed. So the water in an animal's body makes it pressure proof.

Crushed up

Your cabin is full of air, which is a mixture of gases. Unlike liquids, gases can be **compressed**—they will take up less space under pressure. The water outside the sub is pushing on the sphere and squeezing the air inside. If the metal walls of the submarine were not strong enough, they would collapse inward.

★ Comb jellies live in the twilight world at the upper layer of the deep ocean. If a jelly was pulled to the surface, the high-pressure water inside it body would make the animal explode!

★ Even the most modern naval subs rarely dive more than half their **crush depths**. They are not built to travel into the deepest parts of the ocean.

★ CRUSH DEPTH 🐟

Every submarine has a crush depth. A submarine captain never goes this deep because the water pressure down there would be strong enough to break through the craft's walls. Modern navy submarines have a crush depth of about 2,400 feet (730 m), but your submersible can go much deeper than that.

The Big Chill

The surface water near Tenerife was as warm as a swimming pool. Your sensors tell you that it is now a lot cooler.

Temperature drop

As you began your dive, the water **temperature** was 68 °F (20 °C). At 660 feet (200 meters) your **thermometer** shows 59 °F (15 °C), which is still warm enough to swim in. However, by 1,000 feet (300 meters) it has dropped to a chilly 45 °F (7 °C). Down at the edge of the midnight zone there is no light or heat from the Sun to warm the water. The thermometer shows you that the temperature is just 39 °F (4 °C).

★ **ICY FLOW**

In the Arctic and Antarctic oceans, sea water freezes at the surface. The very cold water underneath the ice sinks to the ocean floor. It then flows out around the rest of the world. So a lot of the coldest water in the deep oceans has come all the way from the Arctic and Antarctic.

★ Deep-sea creatures, such as this squid, are **cold blooded**. Their bodies are the same temperature as the water.

Almost freezing

The water in the deep oceans is always cold, even in **tropical** regions. Near the ocean floor the water can be just above freezing temperature. Fresh water freezes at 32 °F (0 °C), but salt water freezes a few degrees lower. A metal flask of drinking water dropped to the seafloor would become solid ice.

Cool effects

The icy water in the deep ocean keeps tropical oceans from getting too hot. If the oceans were hotter, the air above them would be hotter, too. That would make the world's **climate** more extreme.

Lights in the Dark

After your meeting with the cookie-cutter shark, you head back to the surface. However, tomorrow you will dive deeper.

Fade to black

Your next dive will be to 6,600 feet (2,000 meters). As you go deeper the light gets dimmer. You cannot make out colors—everything is a shade of blue. When you reach the midnight zone, there is no light at all. You peer out at the black water—all you can see is your face reflected in the window. Then you switch off the lights inside the sub. You begin to see faint flickers outside.

Lights on

You have trouble making out what is making the light. Then a creature lights up right in front of you— it is a jellyfish. Then just as suddenly the lights go out. The jellyfish has gone.

Glowing lure

★ Small fish think that the anglerfish's **lure** is a tiny bit of food. But before they know it, the anglerfish has gobbled them up.

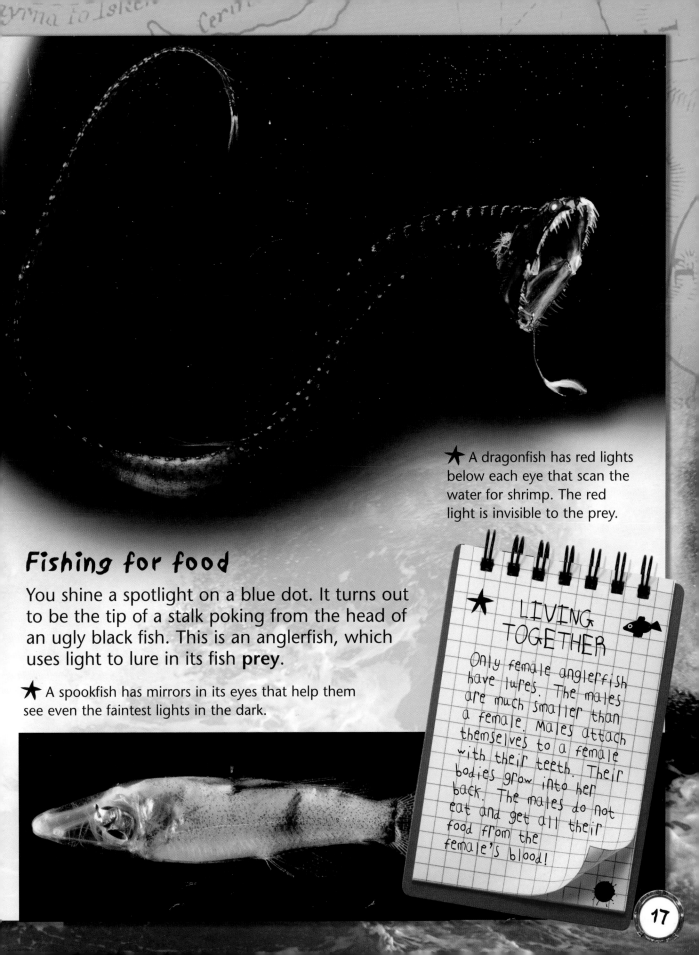

★ A dragonfish has red lights below each eye that scan the water for shrimp. The red light is invisible to the prey.

Fishing for food

You shine a spotlight on a blue dot. It turns out to be the tip of a stalk poking from the head of an ugly black fish. This is an anglerfish, which uses light to lure in its fish **prey**.

★ A spookfish has mirrors in its eyes that help them see even the faintest lights in the dark.

★ LIVING TOGETHER

Only female anglerfish have lures. The males are much smaller than a female. Males attach themselves to a female with their teeth. Their bodies grow into her back. The males do not eat and get all their food from the female's blood!

Weird Fish

During your second dive near Tenerife, you plan to spend three hours in the deep ocean. However, you are finding it difficult to find any fish.

★ Deep-sea fish get few chances to kill and eat prey. They make sure that nothing they catch is able to escape.

Few and far

Deep-sea fish are obviously hard to spot in the dark. However, there is not much food for them down there, so they are usually very spread out as well. The pictures you have seen of some deep-sea hunters look like sea monsters, with huge, needle-shaped teeth. But, most of the fish you do find are only a few inches long. Whatever their size, the fish need to be fierce to survive.

★ A gulper eel (right) can swallow animals that are bigger than its own head.

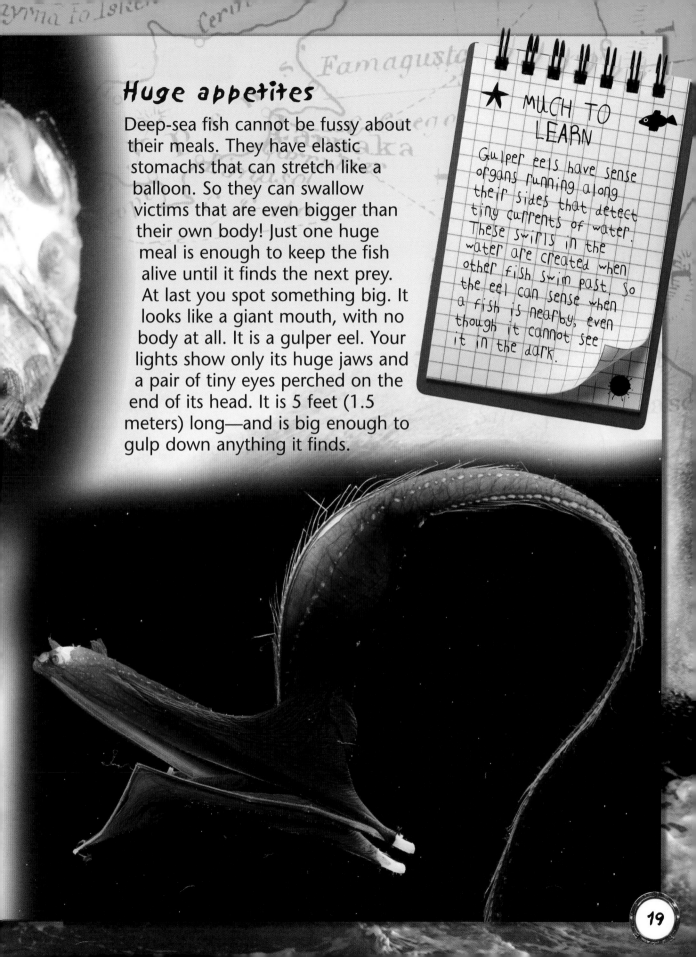

Huge appetites

Deep-sea fish cannot be fussy about their meals. They have elastic stomachs that can stretch like a balloon. So they can swallow victims that are even bigger than their own body! Just one huge meal is enough to keep the fish alive until it finds the next prey. At last you spot something big. It looks like a giant mouth, with no body at all. It is a gulper eel. Your lights show only its huge jaws and a pair of tiny eyes perched on the end of its head. It is 5 feet (1.5 meters) long—and is big enough to gulp down anything it finds.

★ MUCH TO LEARN

Gulper eels have sense organs running along their sides that detect tiny currents of water. These swirls in the water are created when other fish swim past. So the eel can sense when a fish is nearby, even though it cannot see it in the dark.

Looking for Giants

★ Sleeper sharks hunt wherever the water is cold—including down in the deep ocean. They also live in the **polar** seas.

Your research ship is now heading farther out to sea, heading for the cold waters of the North Atlantic. However, first you are going to dive near the Azores Islands.

Hidden mountains

The Azores Islands are part of the Mid-Atlantic Ridge. This is a chain of underwater mountains that runs along the seabed. You head down to see what animals live around the ridge. As expected, there are more fierce fish, but then something much bigger comes into view. It is another shark.

Deep-sea sleeper

This shark is much larger than the little cookie-cutter you saw before. It is a sleeper shark and is as long as two cars. It is the largest fish to live in the midnight zone. How can such a big hunter survive in a place where there is so little food? Sharks can move up and down in the ocean more easily than other fish. So the sleeper shark goes wherever the food is.

★ INVISIBLE ✦ STINGER

A small glowing jellyfish called Periphylla (below) catches shrimp in its stinging tentacles. The jellyfish finds its prey by chance as it floats in the dark.

★ Giant squids have the largest eyes of any animal—they are as wide as plates!

Giant squid

There is an even bigger hunter down here—a giant squid. A giant squid grows to 60 feet (18 meters) long but no one has seen one swimming in the deep. Everything we know about them comes from the squids caught in fishing nets. The squid has huge eyes so they probably look for prey by following the flickering lights of animals in dark water. But no one knows for sure.

Doomed Ship

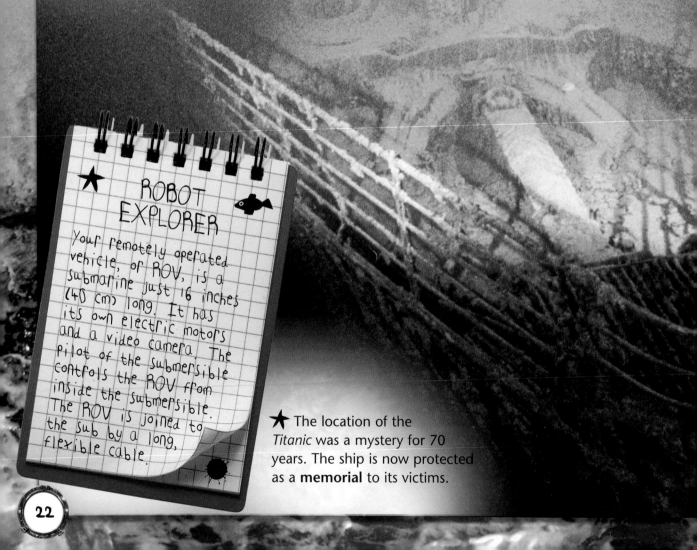

Few people get to visit the deep ocean and return to say what they saw. However, thousands of unlucky sailors have made the journey into the deep—never to return.

One-way trip

Your next dive is a visit to a very famous shipwreck: the *Titanic*. In 1912, the *Titanic* was the most magnificent ocean liner in the world when it made its first voyage across the Atlantic Ocean. But it was also to be the ship's last voyage.

★ ROBOT EXPLORER

Your remotely operated vehicle, or ROV, is a submarine just 16 inches (40 cm) long. It has its own electric motors and a video camera. The pilot of the submersible controls the ROV from inside the submersible. The ROV is joined to the sub by a long, flexible cable.

★ The location of the *Titanic* was a mystery for 70 years. The ship is now protected as a **memorial** to its victims.

Sink to the bottom

Just before midnight on Sunday, April 14th, the *Titanic* hit an iceberg a few hundred miles south of Newfoundland. The ice cut into the side of the ship, which slowly filled with water. In less than three hours the ship sank. It then fell 12,500 feet (3,840 meters) to the dark seabed. Only 705 people survived out of 2,200 passengers and crew.

Lost then found

There were many attempts to find the wreck, but the ship had sunk too deep. In 1985, explorers used remotely operated vehicles (**ROVs**) fitted with cameras to find the giant ship. The ROVs did not have a crew so they could go much deeper than subs. *Titanic* had broken into two parts but was lying upright on the seafloor. Exploring a shipwreck is dangerous. It is easy to get trapped inside. The *Titanic* is huge and there is a lot to explore. You are going to go down to the wreck in the submersible, but you will use an ROV to explore inside.

Rusting Ruin

The *Titanic* is nearly 2.5 miles (4 km) below the ocean surface. It takes two-and-a-half hours to get there.

Down to the wreck

When you get close to the ocean floor, the pilot switches on the powerful headlights and heads for the wreck. Suddenly, in front of you, is the great ship itself. Growing from the wreck are long, rusty spines called **rusticles**. You use the submersible's mechanical hand to snap off some rusticles and put them in the sample basket.

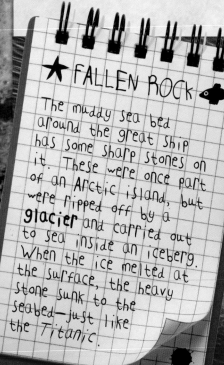

★ FALLEN ROCK

The muddy sea bed around the great ship has some sharp stones on it. These were once part of an Arctic island, but were ripped off by a **glacier** and carried out to sea inside an iceberg. When the ice melted at the surface, the heavy stone sunk to the seabed—just like the *Titanic*.

Into the hull

You head toward the ship's **bridge**. That is where the captain would have stood as it sank. You guide the ROV through a smashed window. and send it deep into the ship to where the ice ripped the hull. There are only small gashes in the side of the ship, covering just 12 square feet (1.1 square meters). All the water that sank the liner came through a hole the size of a bathtub.

Iron eaters

Back in the ship's lab on your return to the research ship, you examine the rust sample. The rusticle is full of tiny **bacteria**. They have made themselves a home in the rusting ship. It seems that the deep-sea bacteria are eating the *Titanic*'s iron. Eventually the bacteria will eat so much iron that the giant wreck will collapse into a heap of rusty sludge.

★ The *Titanic* had three immense propellers. Even these huge pieces of iron will one day disappear.

Rusticle

At the Bottom

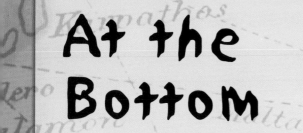

Hatch

Your next dive will be in the Pacific—into Earth's deepest water.

Touch down

You submersible has been carried by air to the island of Guam. From there it is a short voyage to the Mariana Trench. The deepest point in the trench is called the Challenger Deep. It is nearly 7 miles (11 km) deep!

Cabin

Window

Trench

Challenger Deep

★ The Mariana Trench formed when a piece of **Earth's crust** plunged down underneath another piece.

★ The only people to reach Challenger Deep traveled in the *Trieste* in 1960. This deep-sea submersible had a tiny cabin under floats containing gasoline and water, and tanks of iron pellets used for weight.

★ **MARINE SNOW**

There is very little food in the deepest parts of the ocean. Most of the things that live in ocean trenches eat marine snow. This is the scraps of dead animals that sink from the water above to form a layer of slime on the seabed.

At the bottom

It will take more than 6 hours to reach the seabed. It is deeper than the highest mountain, Everest, is tall. At this depth, the water pressure is huge. The weight of a car is pushing down on every square inch of the sub's surface.

Lonely journey

Your submersible is only the second craft to carry a crew into Challenger Deep. You are a little nervous as you climb aboard—but that changes to excitement as you near the seabed. You hear a slight crunch, and feel the craft settle on the floor of the ocean trench. You are in the deepest hole on Earth.

Anything out there?

You switch on the outside lights. A slimy layer of **marine snow** lies on the seabed. There are several strange grooves in the slime. The grooves are probably the tracks of animals called sea cucumbers. So there is life even down here, in the deepest part of the ocean.

Lessons We've Learned

You may not have liked the feeling of being miles beneath the surface, but the view out of the thick windows has always made the trip worthwhile.

Tough times

Diving to the deep ocean was exhausting work. It took a long time to get there, cramped in a tiny submersible—and you only had a few minutes to explore before it was time to head home.

Weird sights

You saw some amazing fish and other animals, including many that glow in the dark. You discovered how they find prey with their sharp senses and light tricks. And now you know how they use their big mouths and long teeth to catch prey.

★ **Seamounts** are usually volcanoes.

★ SEAMOUNTS
Diving into the deep-sea is dangerous. Even if you think you are heading into open water you might get a surprise. The seabed is covered in mountains called seamounts. And we still do not know where they all are. Submarine pilots are always on the look out, or they might crash into the side of a mountain!

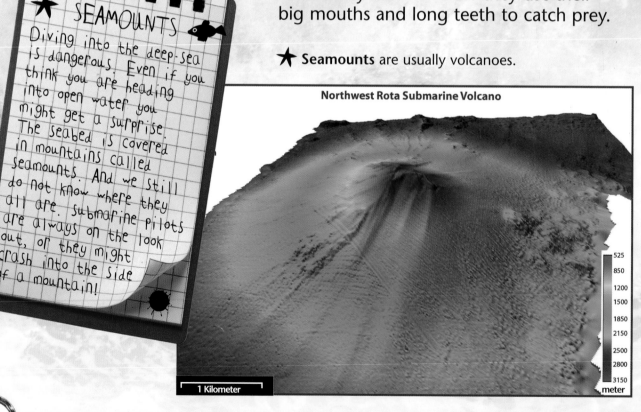

Northwest Rota Submarine Volcano

1 Kilometer

525
850
1200
1500
1850
2150
2500
2800
3150
meter

★ A black swallower is a deep-sea fish with a gigantic mouth. It is capable of eating prey even larger than itself.

Cold ruin

In the North Atlantic you sailed over underwater mountains and visited the wreck of the *Titanic*. You discovered how it sank in 1912, and what has happened to it during a century on the seabed.

Going deep

In the Pacific you took a trip to the deepest part of any ocean, anywhere on Earth. You found that life lives even there. It has been an amazing journey, one that few people will get a chance to make.

Glossary

bacteria very small living things that reproduce by splitting in two

bridge on a ship, the control center where the captain usually works

climate weather of a place over a whole year

cold blooded describing an animal that is always the same temperature as its surroundings

compressed squashed

crush depth the deepest a submarine can go before it is crushed by the water

current flow of ocean water

Earth's crust the rocky shell that covers the planet's surface

extinct no longer existing (animals and plants), or no longer active (volcanoes)

glacier sheets of ice found in mountain valleys or very cold regions

lure bait that can be used again and again

marine snow tiny pieces of dead animals and plants that sink from the surface into deep water

memorial something that honors people who died in a tragedy

midnight zone the area of the deep ocean where light never reaches

organs parts of living things with special jobs to do. The heart and lungs are organs.

polar relating to the North or South Pole

pressure squeezing force produced by a heavy weight. Pressure is a measure by the force pushing on a fixed area.

prey animals that are killed and eaten by other animals

ROV Remotely Operated Vehicle. It is a small underwater craft that is steered by someone sitting in another craft.

rusticles icicle-like growths made of rust and tiny living things. They form on iron in the deep ocean.

seamounts volcanoes that have erupted from the ocean floor, but have not grown tall enough to reach the surface

submersible small submarine designed for short trips. Some can dive to great depths.

temperature a measure of how hot something is

tentacles flexible "arms" used by squid or jellyfish to catch prey

thermometer instrument that measures temperature

tropical of the tropics, a region near the equator, where it is always warm

twilight gloomy light, such as the sunlight at dawn or dusk

water pressure force of water pressing down on something

Further Information

Books

Exploring the Ocean Depths: The Final Frontier. Mankato, MN: Smart Apple Media, 2003.

Glow in the Dark Book of Ocean Creatures by Nicholas Harris. Brookfield, CN: Millbrook Press, 2002.

Oceans: The Vast, Mysterious Deep by David L. Harrison. Honesdale, PA: Boyds Mills Press, 2003.

Web sites

Games and videos from the BBC's Blue Planet site.
http://www.bbc.co.uk/nature/blueplanet/

National Oceanic and Atmospheric Administration Ocean Explorer.
http://oceanexplorer.noaa.gov/

An animated fly-through of the Mariana Trench from the National Geophysical Data Center (NGDC)
http://www.ngdc.noaa.gov/mgg/image/marianas.html

An excellent web site about the famous wreck.
http://www.titanic-online.com/

Index